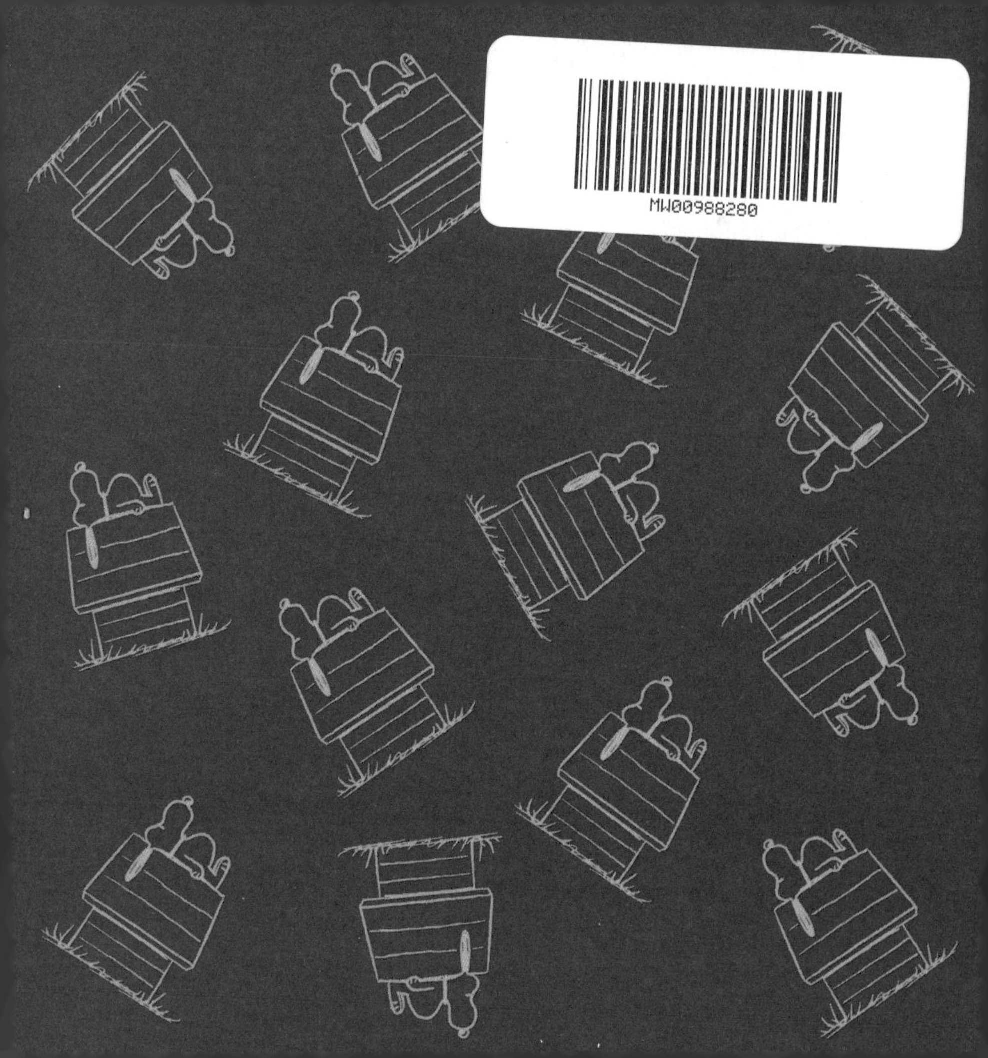

# SUPPER TIME!
## BY
## CHARLES M. SCHULZ

ISBN-13: 978-1-933662-38-1
ISBN-10: 1-933662-38-7

This book may be ordered by mail from the publisher.
Please include $4.50 for postage and handling.
**But please support your local bookseller first!**

Books published by Cider Mill Press Book Publishers are available at special discounts
for bulk purchases in the United States by corporations, institutions, and other
organizations. For more information, please contact the publisher.

Cider Mill Press Book Publishers
"Where good books are ready for press"
12 Port Farm Road
Kennebunkport, Maine 04046

Visit us on the web!
*www.cidermillpress.com*

Design by: Jason Zamajtuk

Printed in China

1 2 3 4 5 6 7 8 9 10

A PEANUTS CLASSIC Edition

# SUPPER TIME!

# IT MUST BE SUPPERTIME... MY STOMACH-CLOCK JUST WENT OFF!

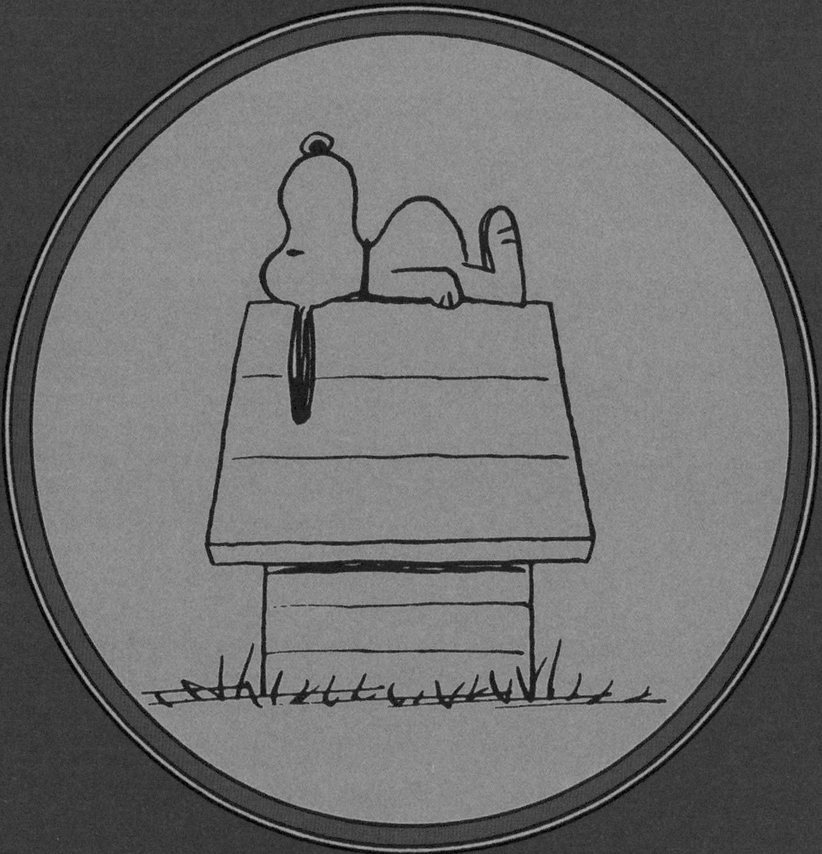

**T**HREE HUNDRED AND FIFTY MILLION DOLLARS A YEAR IS SPENT ON DOG FOOD! I WONDER IF THAT INCLUDES TIPS!

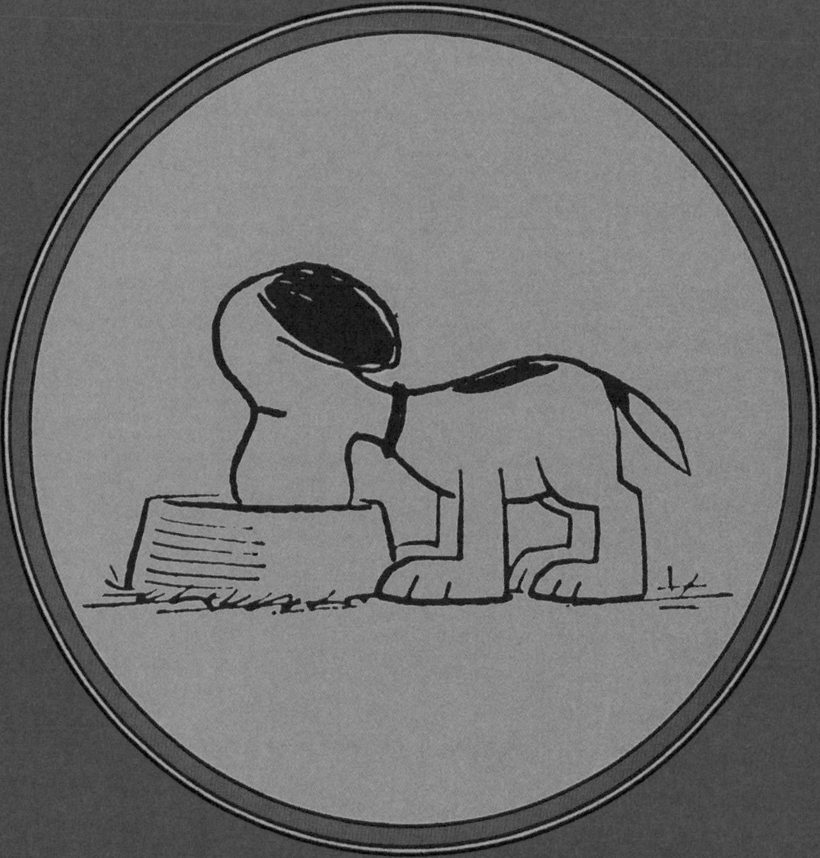

# No

# AFTER-DINNER

# SPEAKER?

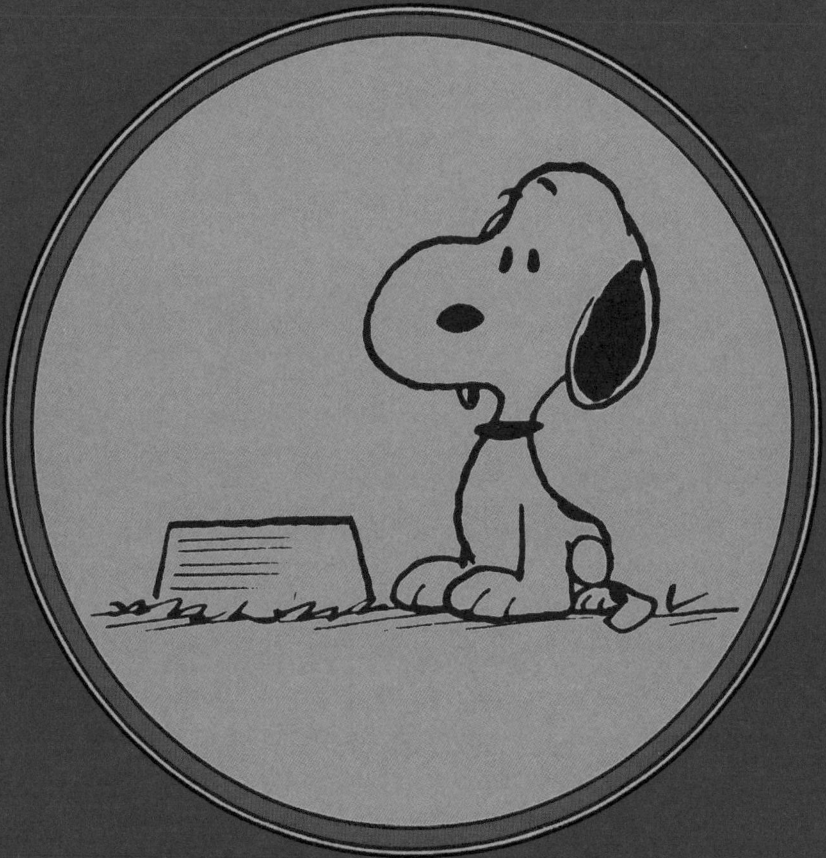

**T**HIS IS GOOD HOT CHOCOLATE, BUT IT WOULD TASTE EVEN BETTER WITH A SKI LODGE AROUND IT!

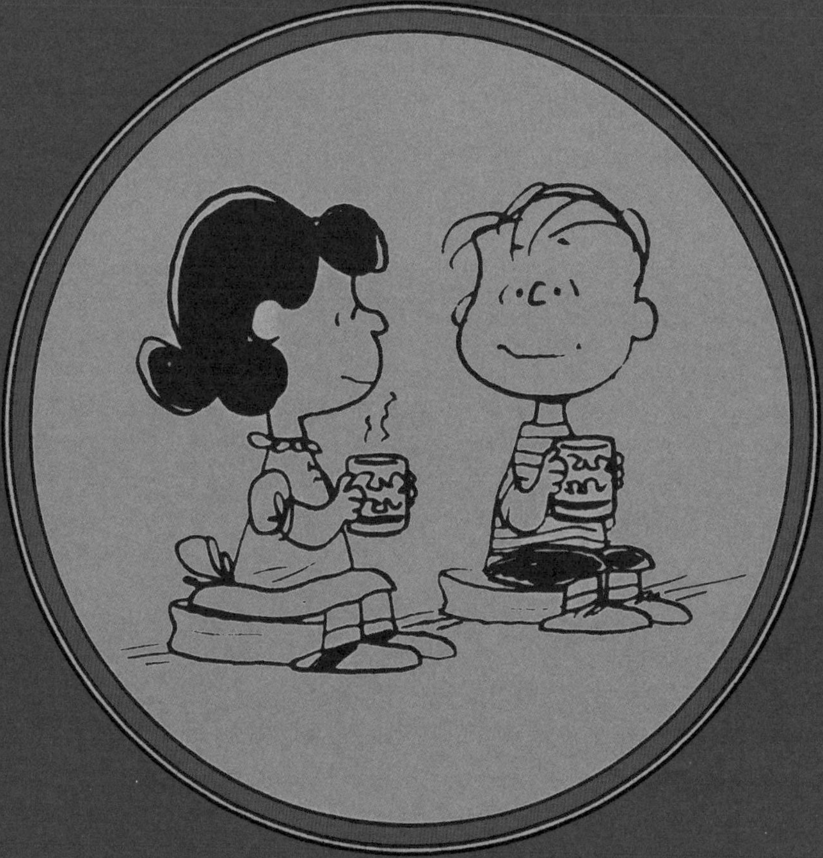

TO ME, THE UGLIEST SIGHT IN THE WORLD IS AN EMPTY DOG DISH!

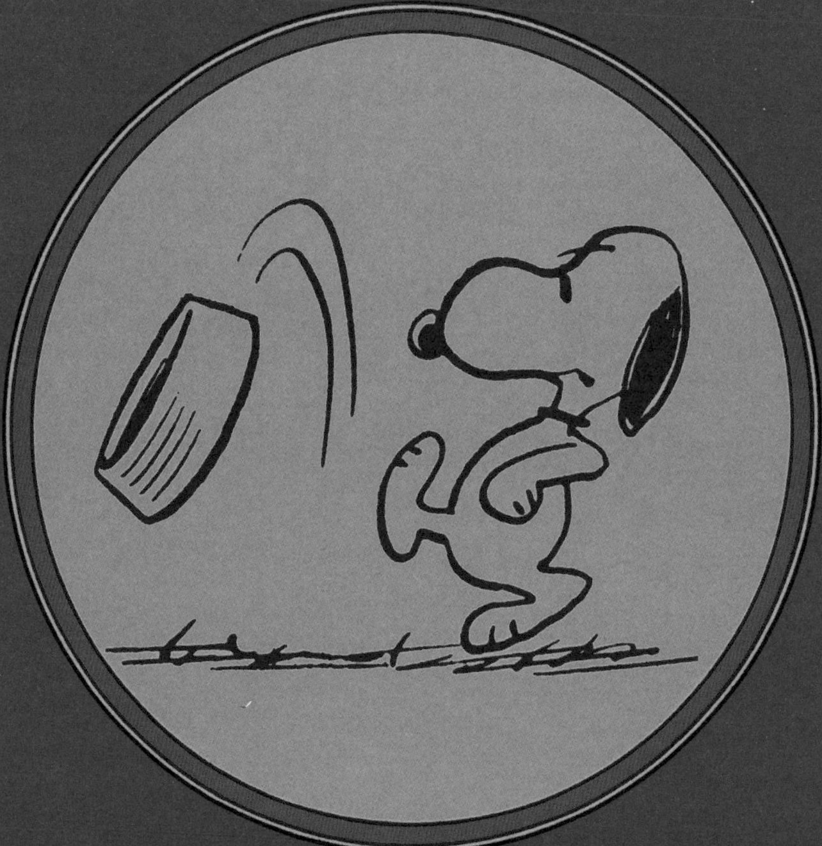

# A
# WATCHED
# SUPPER DISH
# NEVER
# FILLS!

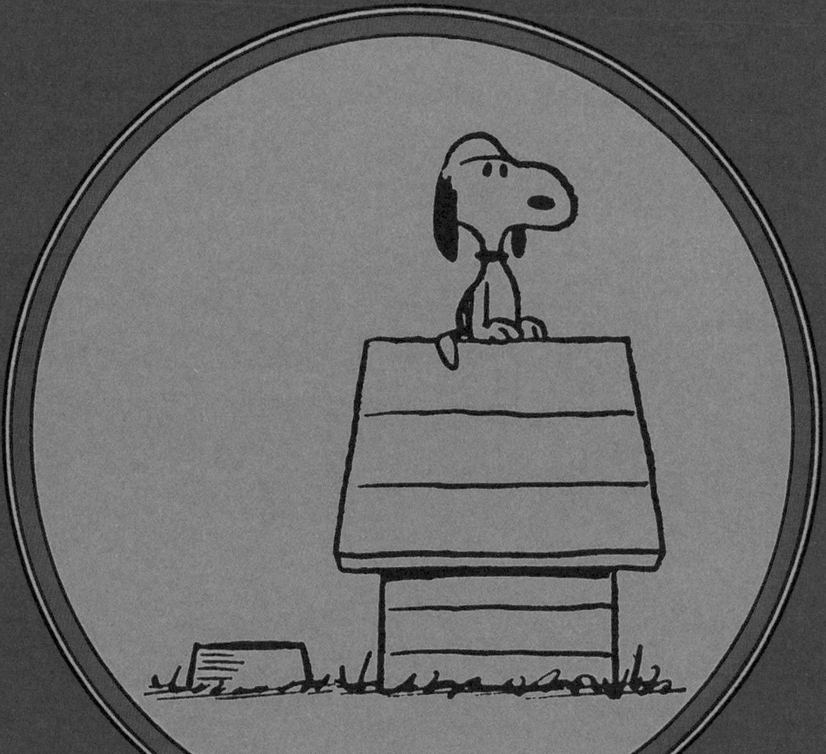

# My
## STOMACH
## TELLS ME IT'S
## SUPPERTIME BUT
## I KNOW IT ISN'T.
## I HATE
## A STOMACH
## THAT TELLS
## LIES!

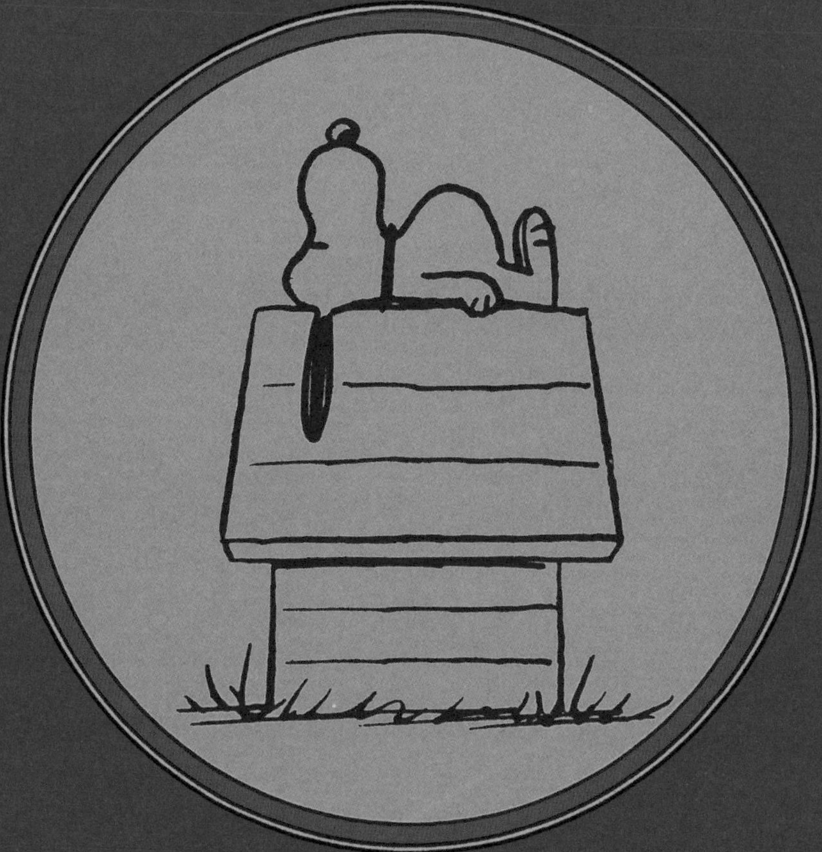

# WITHHOLD MY COMPLIMENTS TO THE CHEF!

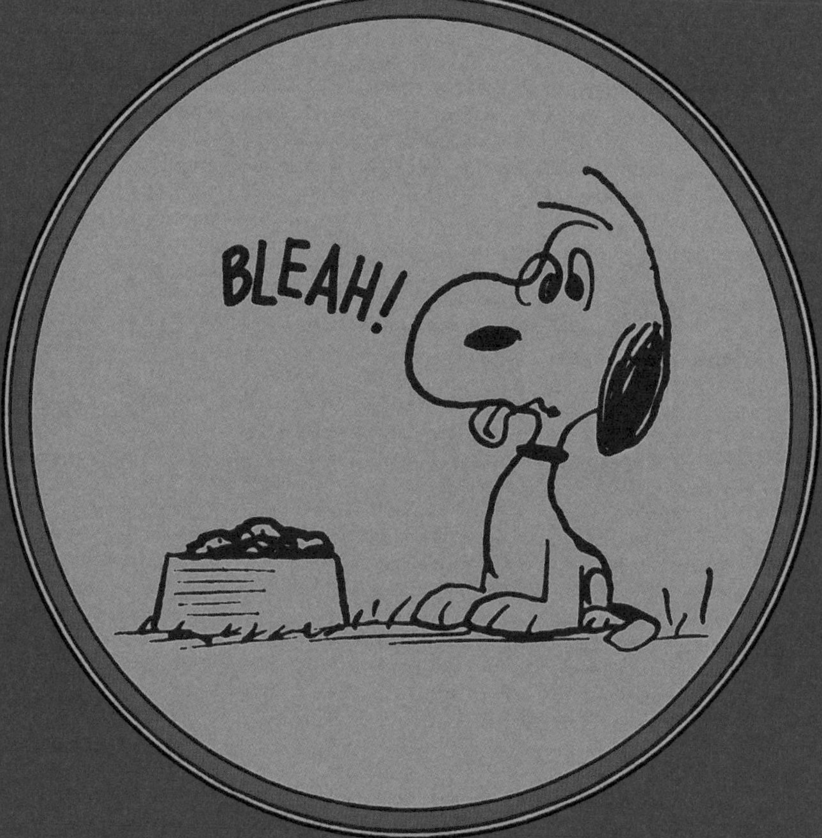
BLEAH!

# I KNOW YOU HAVE A COLD, SO I PUT A MENTHOL COUGH DROP ON TOP!

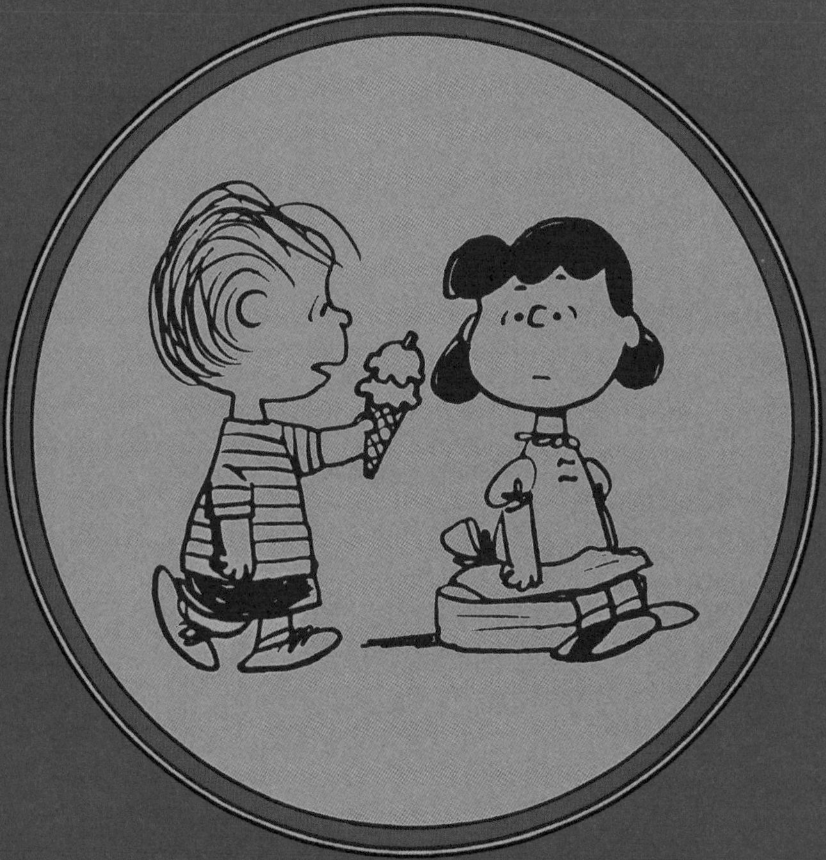

# ACTUALLY, WORLD WAR I FLYING ACES VERY SELDOM DRANK ROOT BEER.

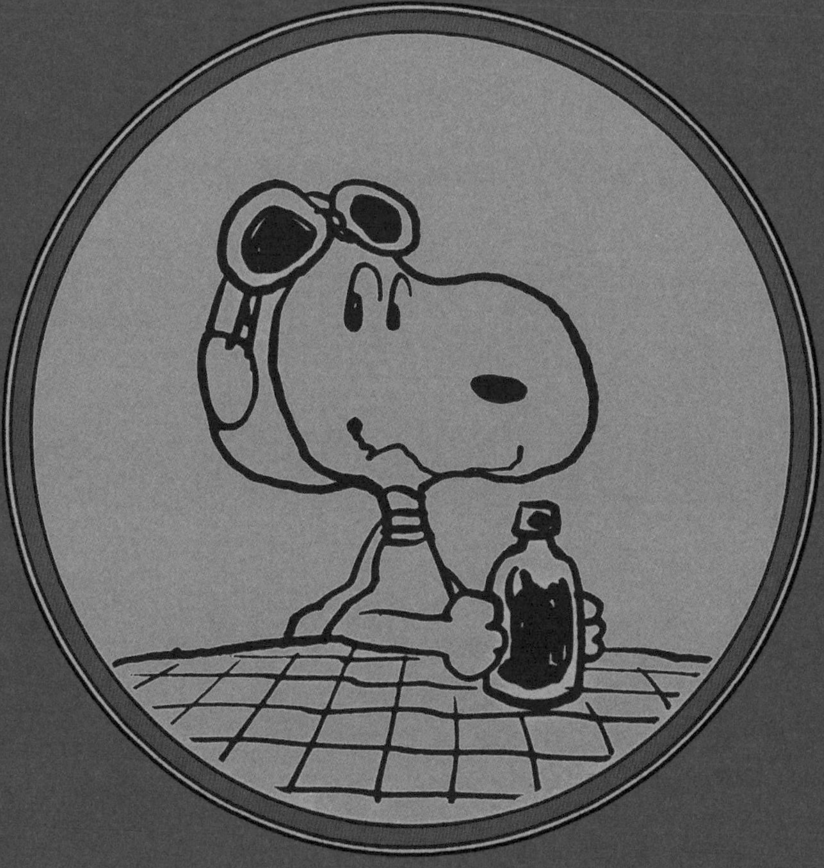

# I KNEW I SMELLED A PICNIC GOING BY!

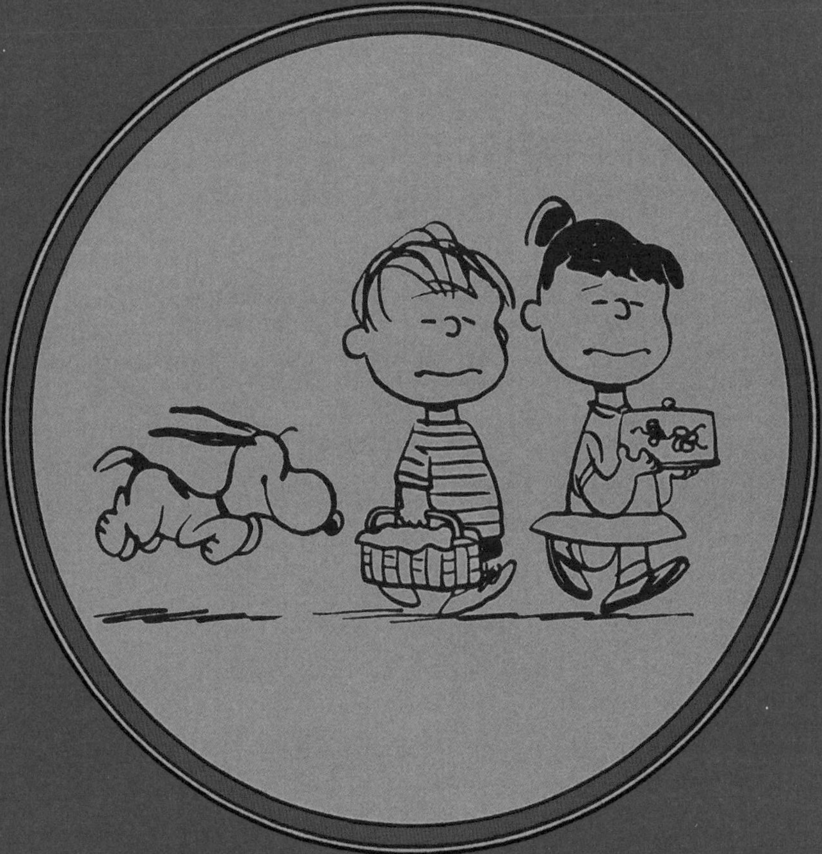

# I HATE IT WHEN IT SNOWS ON MY FRENCH TOAST!

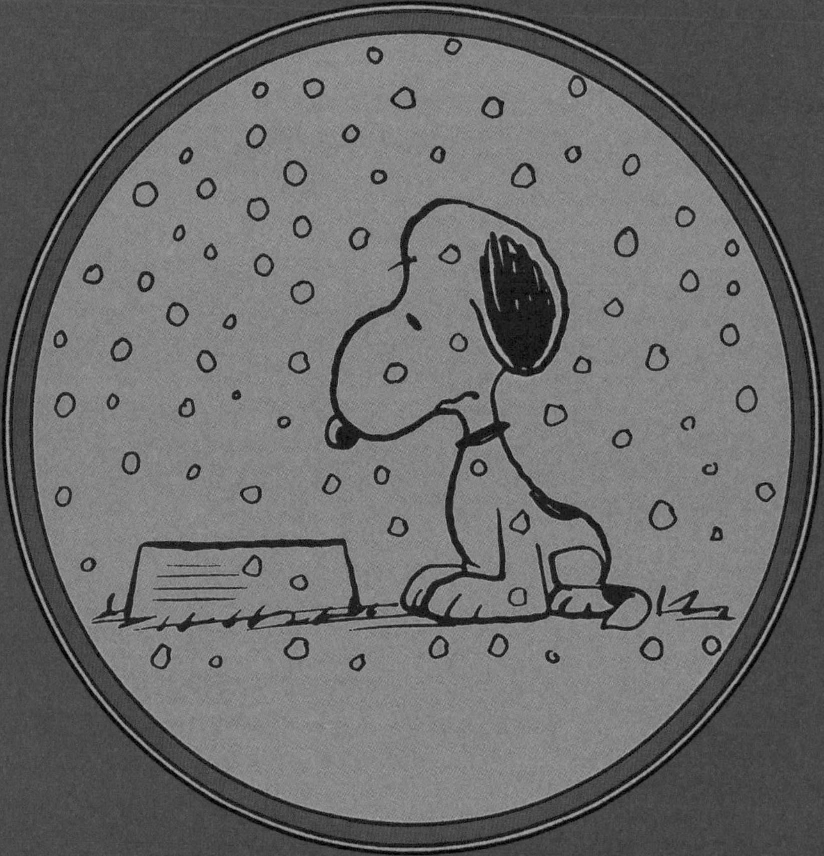

# Roquefort or Thousand Island?

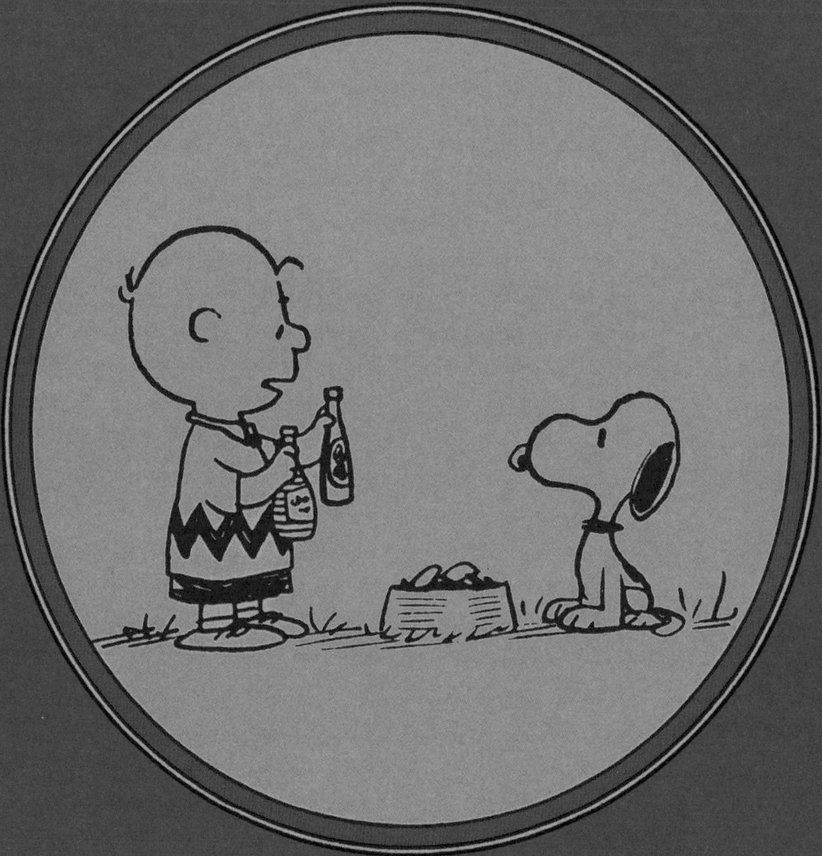

# I'VE JUST GOT TO KEEP EATING UNTIL I'VE FORGOTTEN OL' "WHAT'S-HER-NAME"?

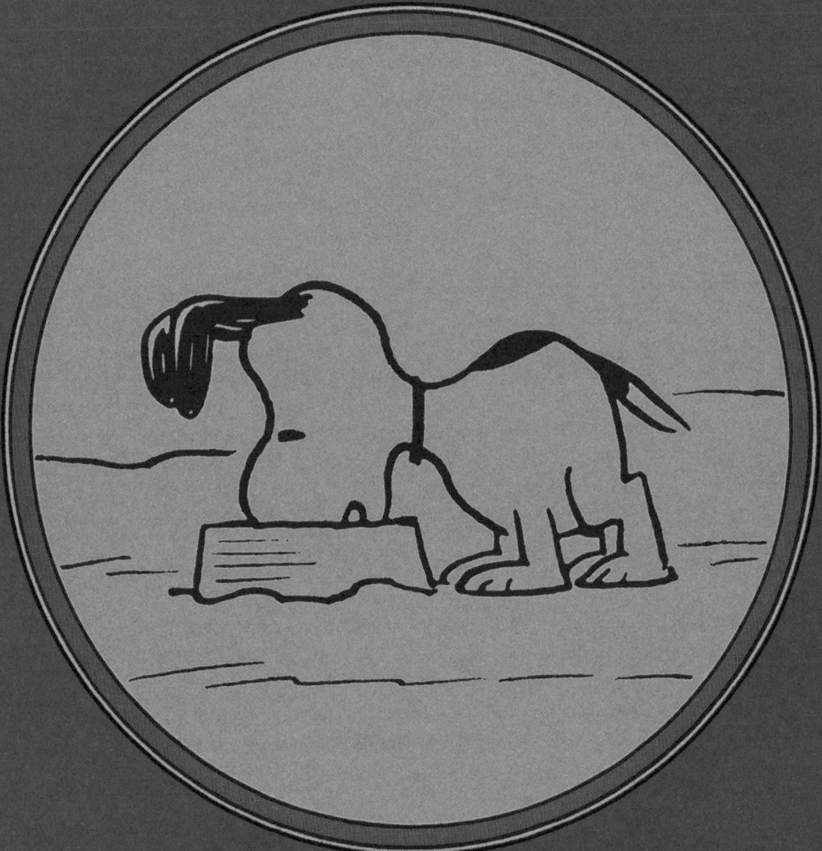

# Twenty-three pounds... How humiliating!

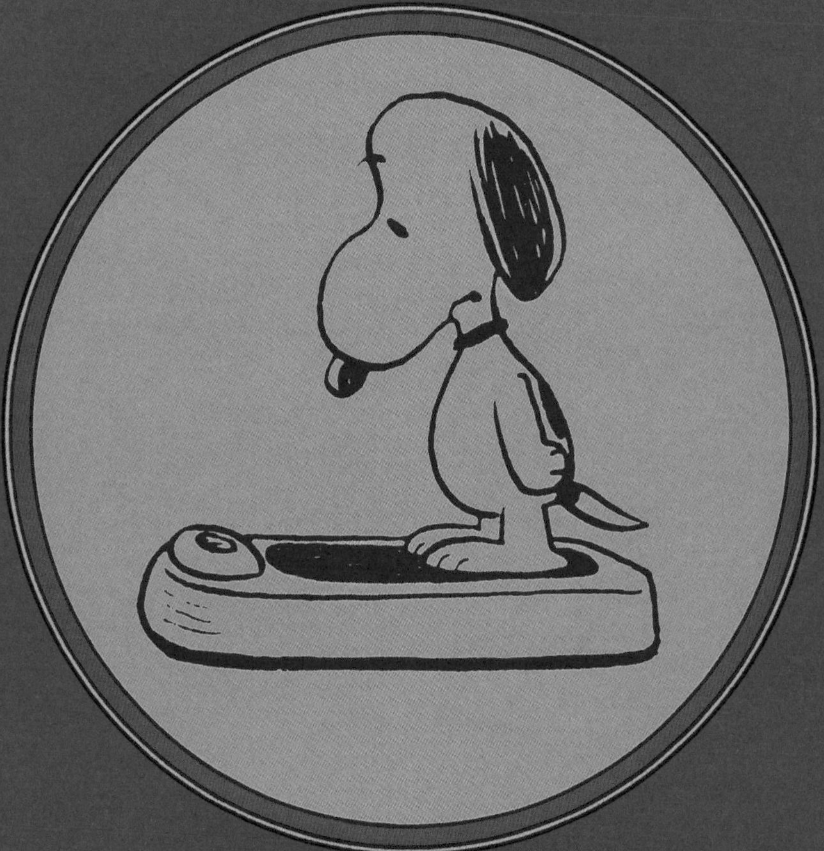

# EATING OUT CAN BE FUN!

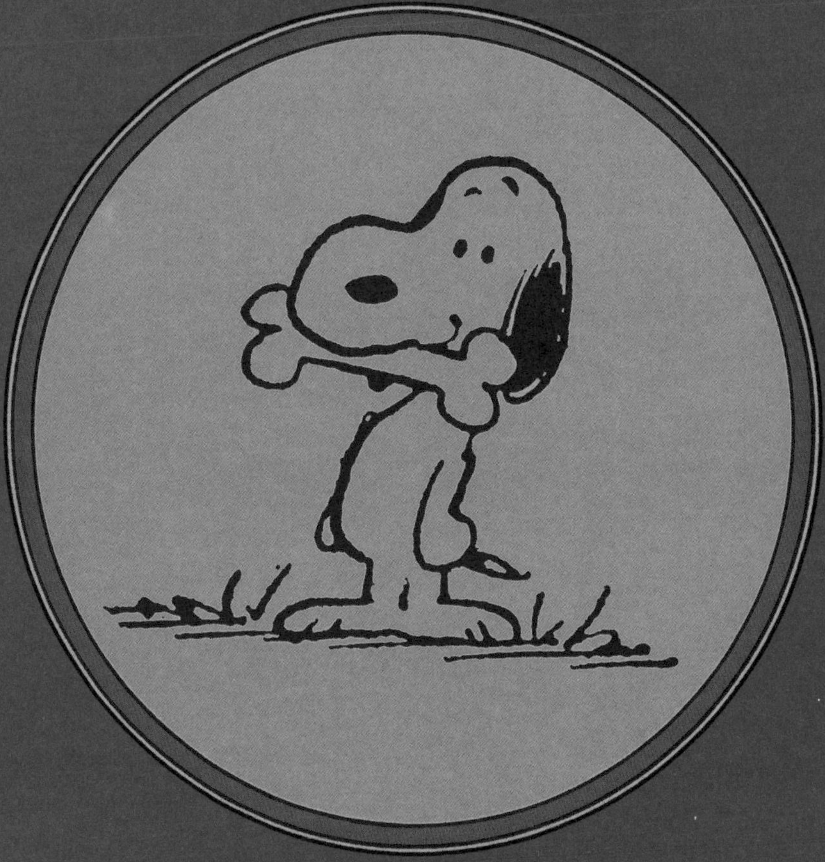

# THUMB
# A
# LA
# MODE!

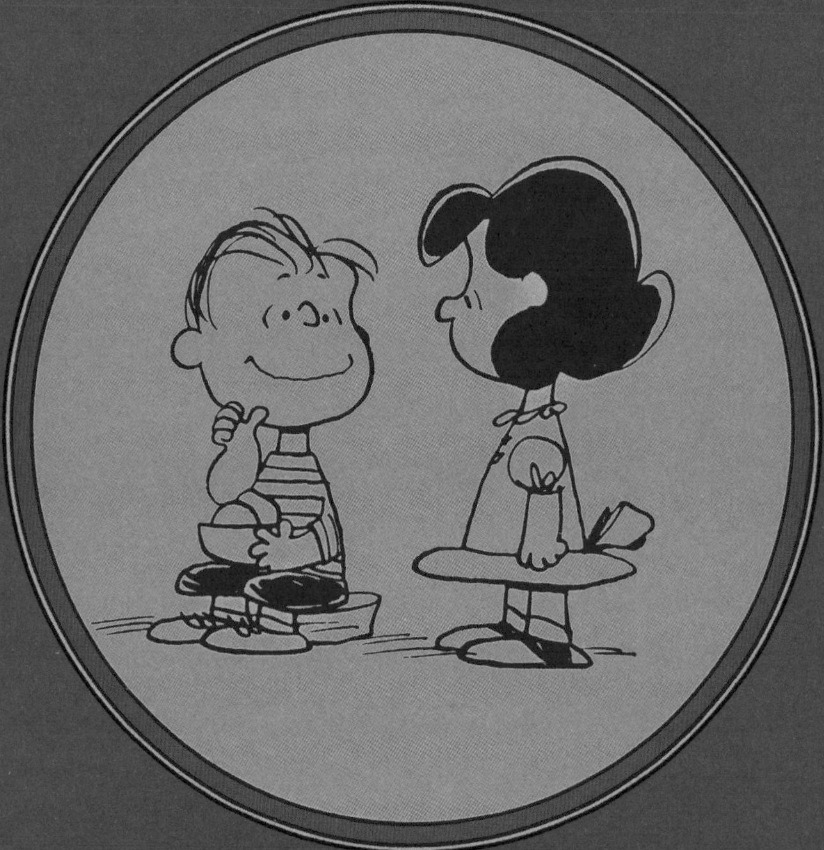

# IT'S THE MIDDLE OF JANUARY! IT'S SNOWING! THE WEATHER IS FREEZING! ...AND WHAT DO I GET? COLD CEREAL.

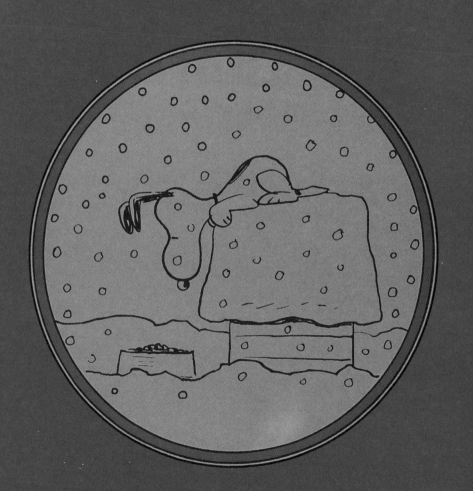

TONIGHT
I THINK I'LL HAVE
MY SUPPER IN THE
YELLOW DISH AND
MY DRINKING WATER
IN THE RED DISH...
LIFE IS TOO SHORT
NOT TO LIVE IT UP
A LITTLE!

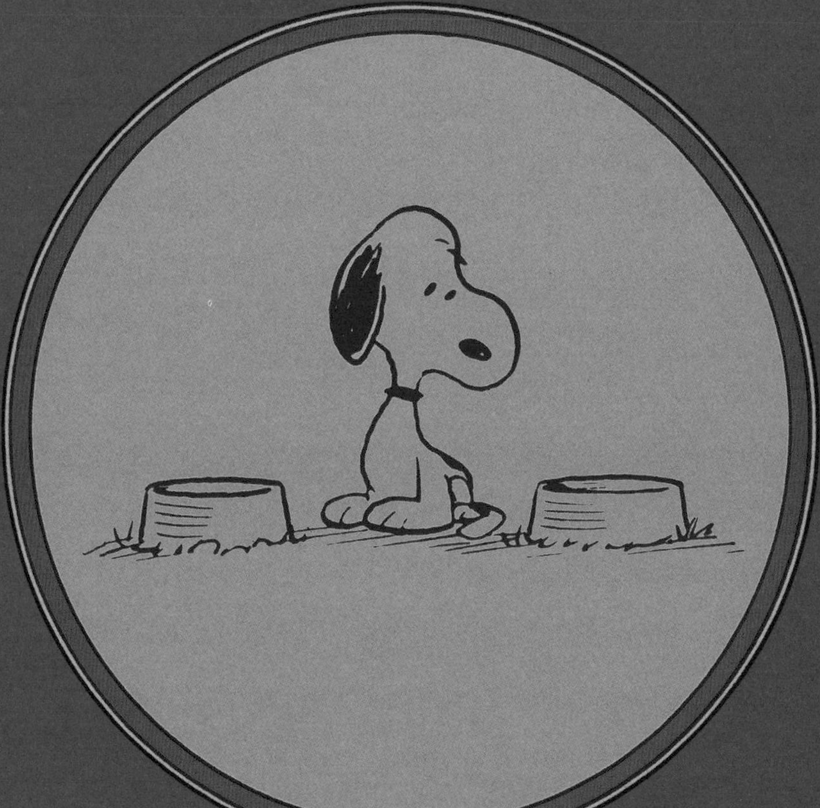

# I WAS SITTING HERE WATCHING T.V., WHEN ALL OF A SUDDEN, I FELT A PIECE OF JELLY BREAD CALLING ME!

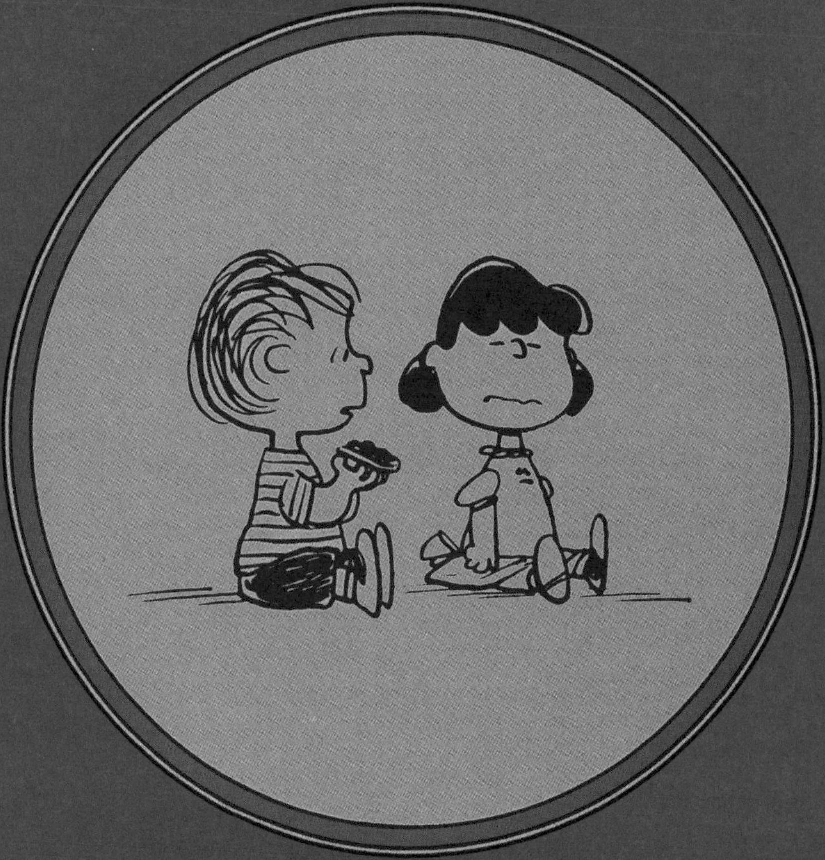

# A GOOD WAY TO FORGET A LOVE AFFAIR IS TO EAT A LOT OF GOOP!

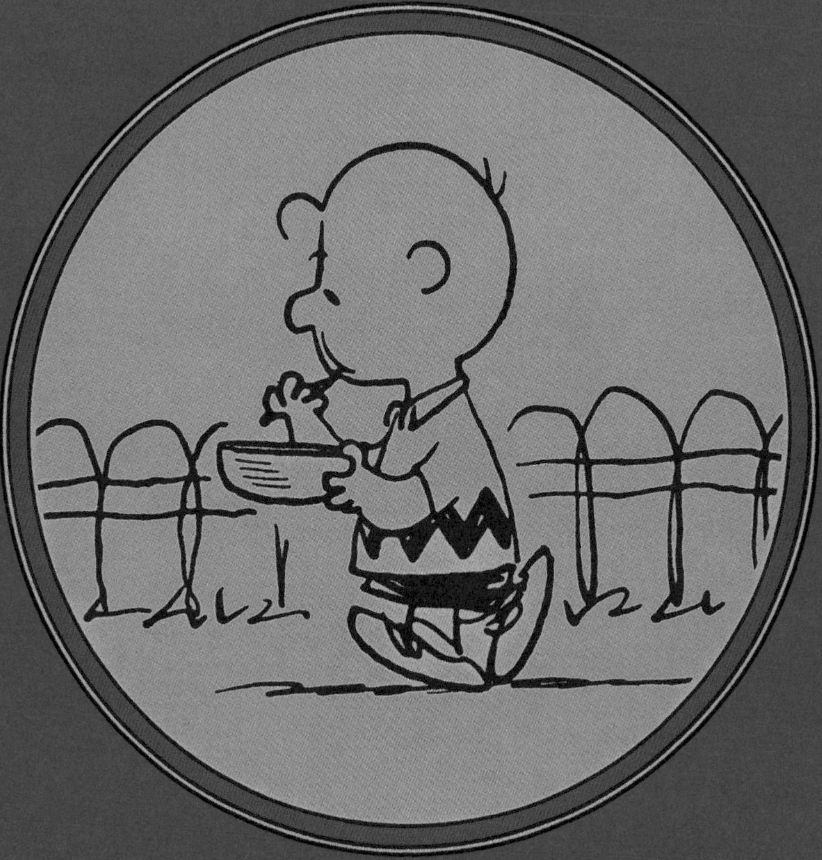

# I NEVER KNOW WHAT TO DO WITH THE USED TEA BAG...

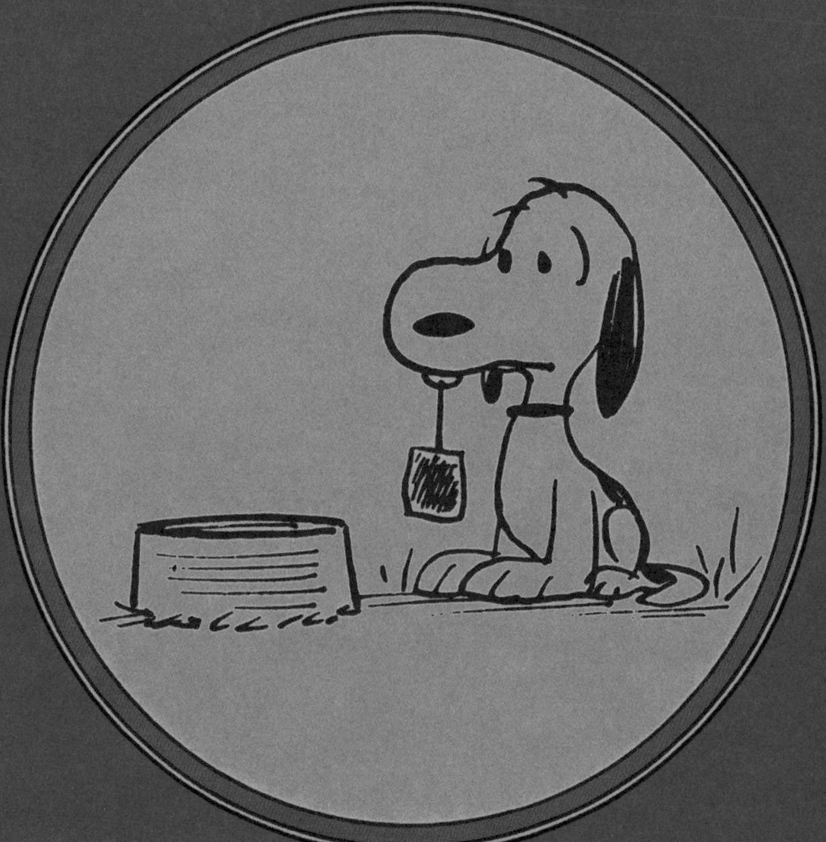

# CRITICIZE ME ALL YOU WANT, BUT DON'T INTERFERE WITH MY FOOD-LIFE!

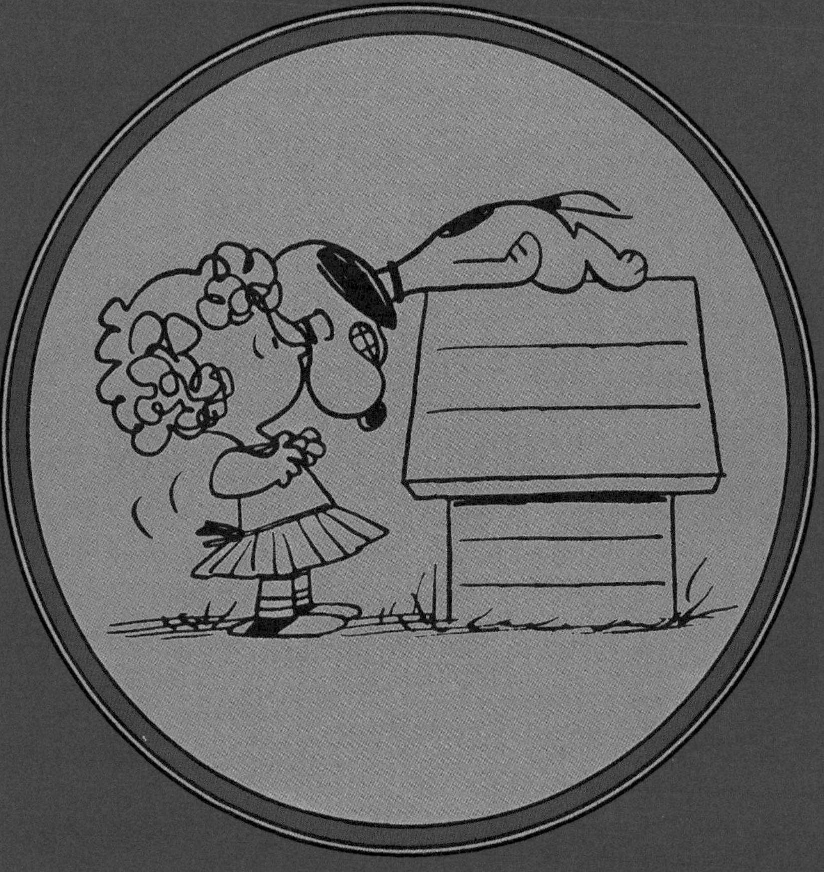

# I
## LOVE EATING IN A CAFETERIA... I'LL HAVE SOME OF THIS, AND SOME OF THAT, AND SOME OF THESE AND SOME OF THOSE!

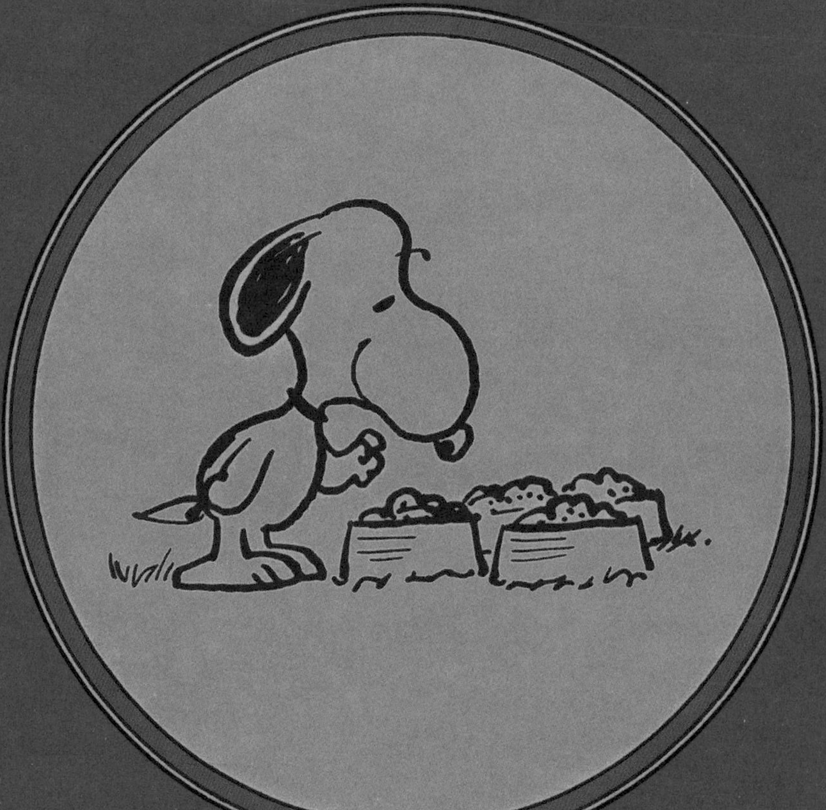

# JUST AS I THOUGHT, HE'S CUTTING DOWN MY RATIONS!

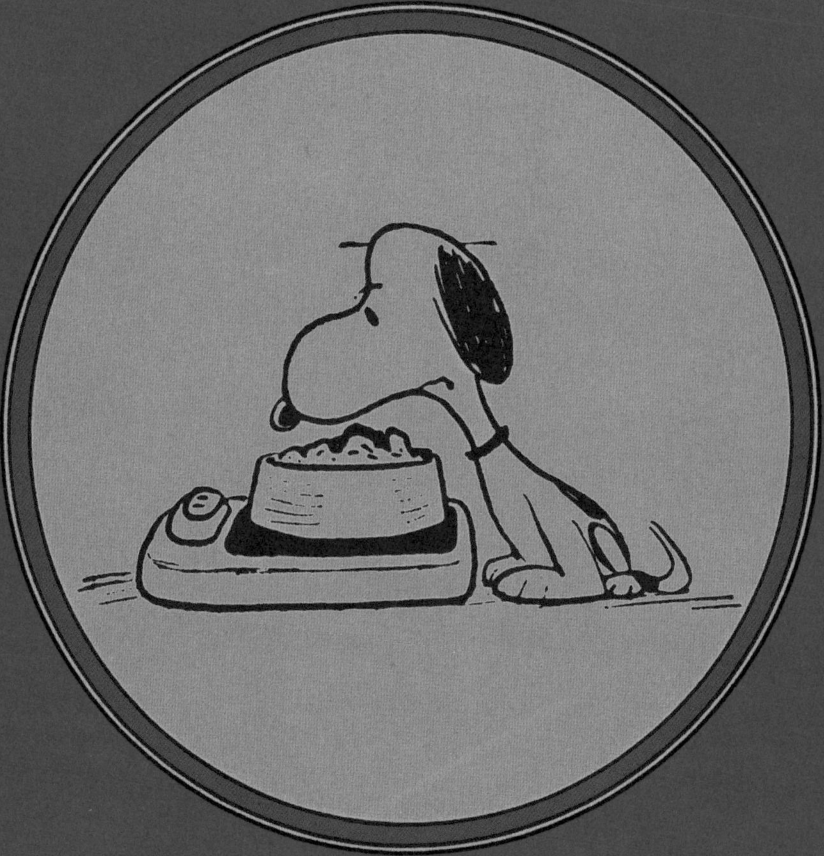

THAT'S THE ONLY DOG I KNOW WHO WORRIES ABOUT HIS CHOLESTEROL LEVEL!

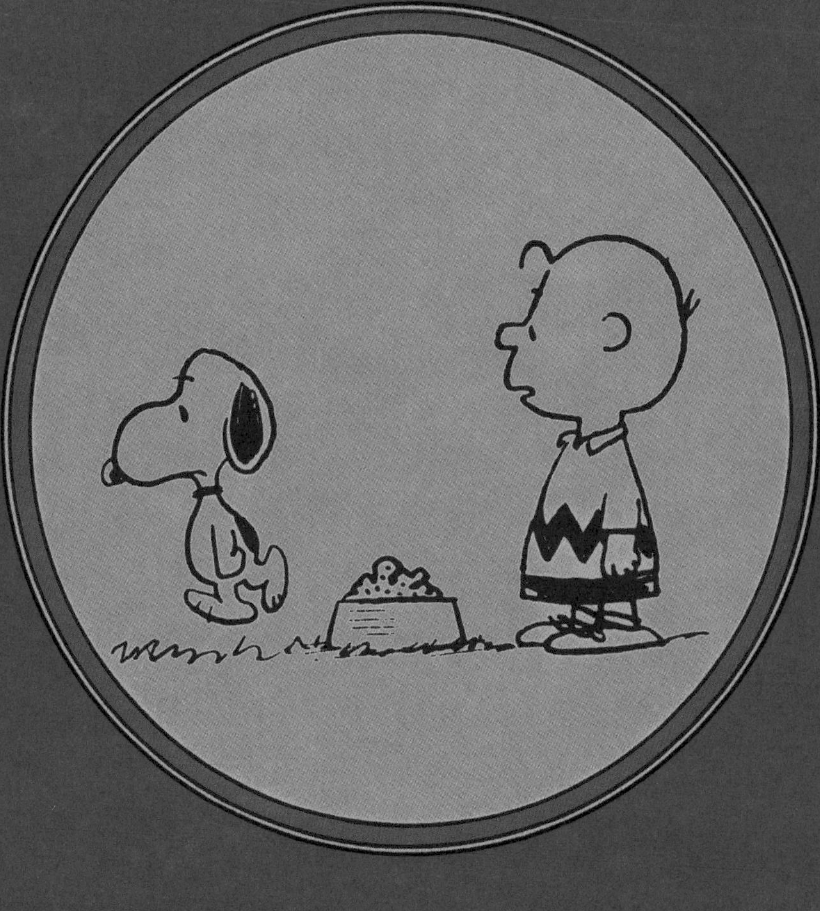

CHRISTMAS HAS BEEN OVER FOR TWO MONTHS AND I'M STILL GETTING " FIGGY PUDDING "!

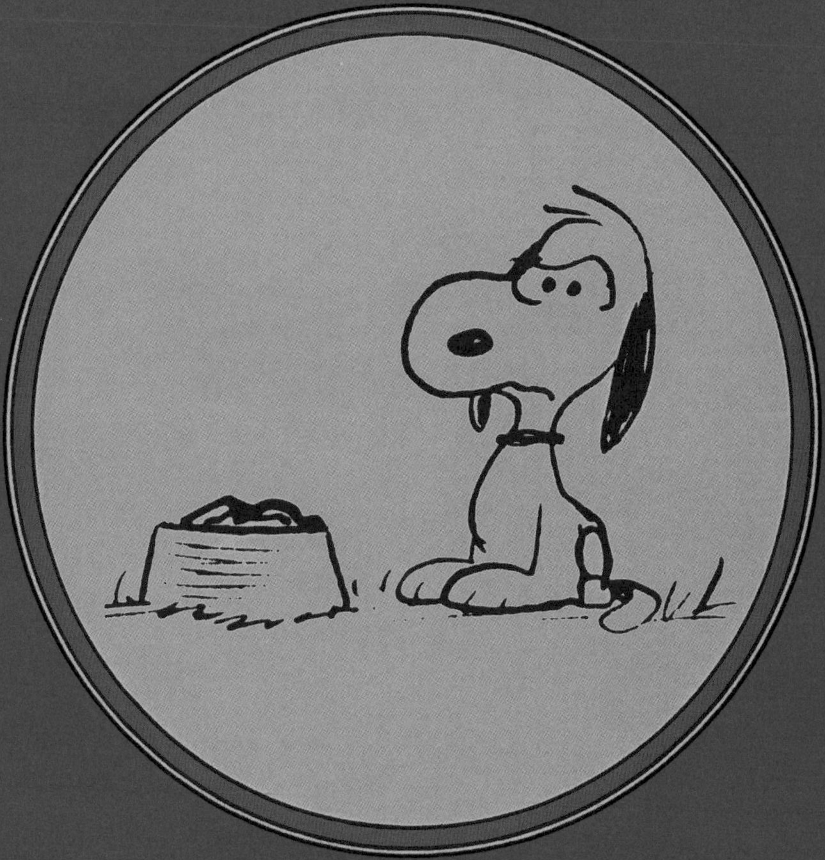

# I EAT BECAUSE I'M FRUSTRATED... AND I'M FRUSTRATED BECAUSE I DON'T GET TO EAT ENOUGH!

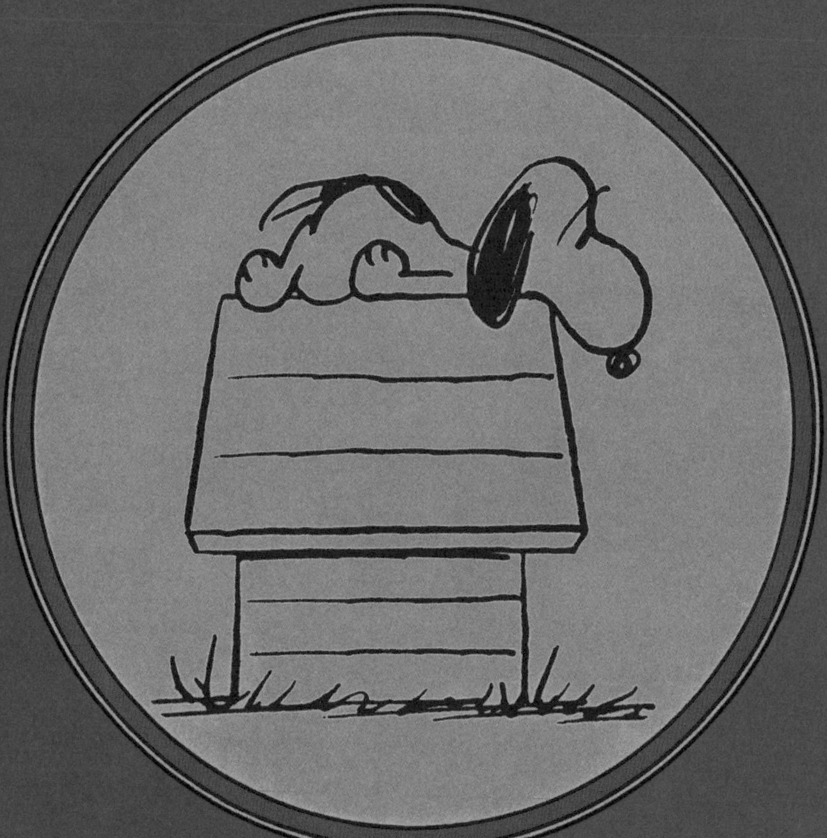

# Rats...

## HE ALWAYS PUTS TOO MUCH CINNAMON ON MY CINNAMON TOAST!

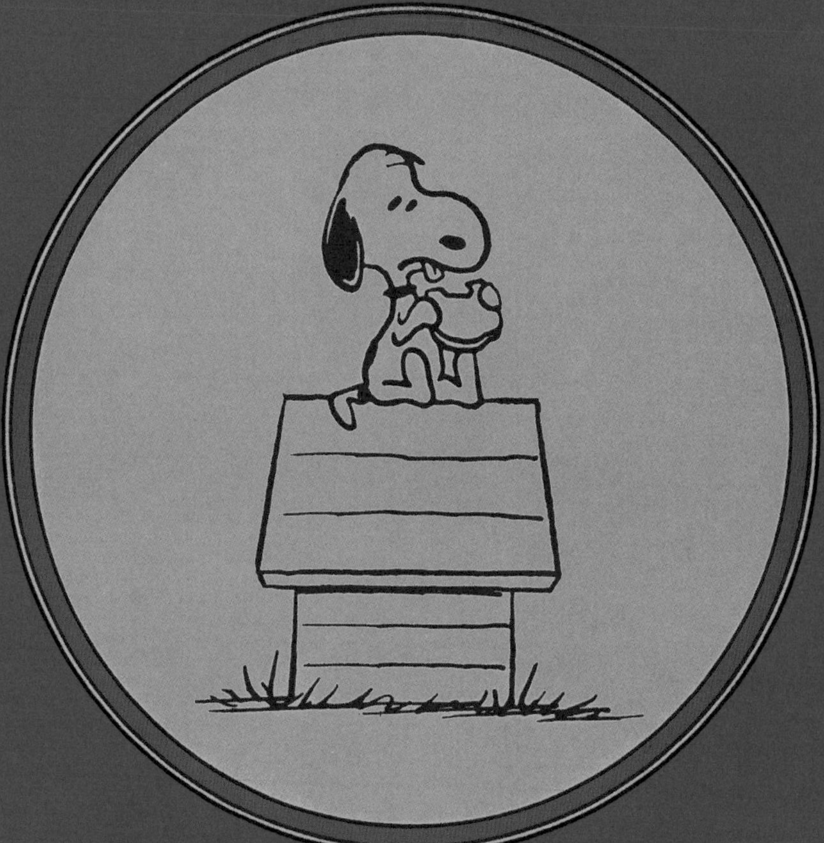

# How can I eat when I feel guilty?

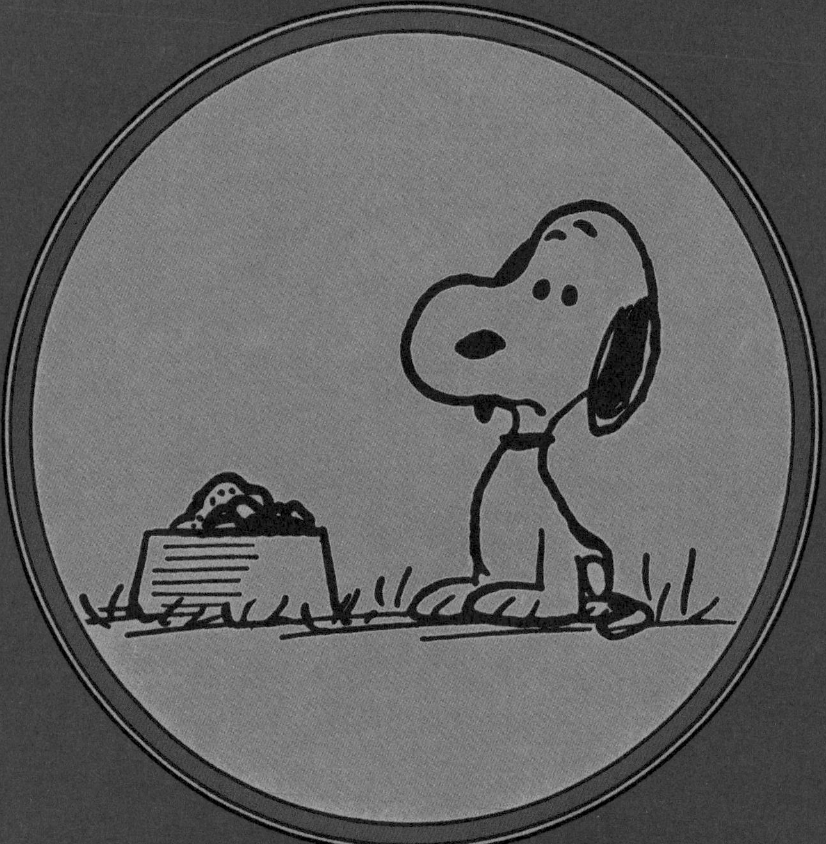

## Other Books by Charles M. Schulz

Happiness Is A Warm Puppy

Home Is On Top of A Dog House

Security Is A Thumb and A Blanket

Happiness Is A Sad Song

Love Is Walking Hand In Hand

I Need All The Friends I Can Get

Christmas Is Together-Time

## About Cider Mill Press Book Publishers

Good ideas ripen with time. From seed to harvest, Cider Mill Press strives to bring fine reading, information, and entertainment together between the covers of its creatively crafted books. Our Cider Mill bears fruit twice a year, publishing a new crop of titles each Spring and Fall.

*Visit us on the web at*
www.cidermillpress.com
*or write to us at*
12 Port Farm Road
Kennebunkport, Maine 04046

*Where Good Books are
Ready for Press*

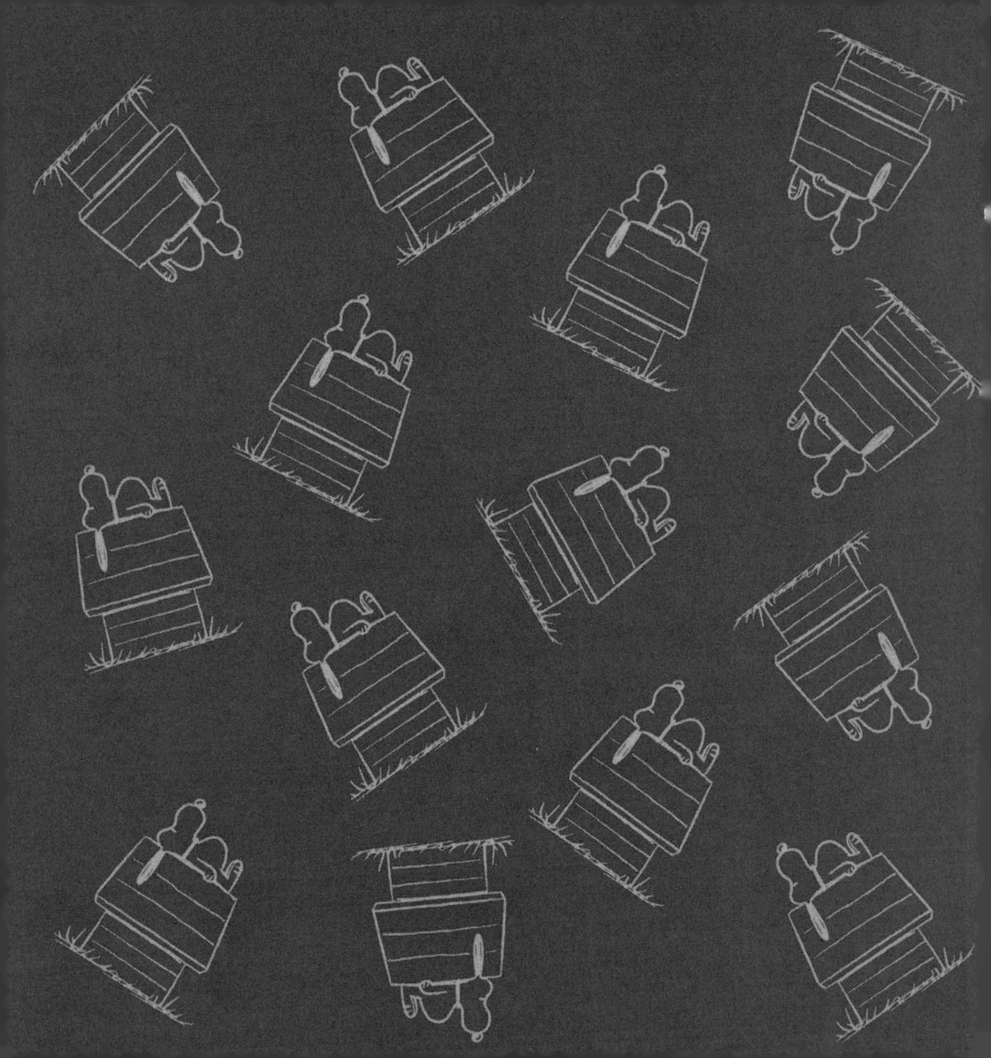